ON THE DATING OF ENGLISH ... FROM EXTERNAL EVIDENCE

By J. T. SMITH
Royal Commission on Historical Monuments
and E. M. YATES
Department of Geography, Kings College, London

There are three things that make man forcefully
To flee from his own house, as Holywrit shows us.
One is a wicked wife, who will not be chastened;
Her man flees from her for fear of her revilings.
If his house becomes uncovered and it rain on his pallet,
He seeks and seeks till he can sleep dry.
And when smoke and smother strike his eyesight,
It is worse than his wife and a wet blanket.

> *Vision of Piers Ploughman*
> Passus XVIII, 325–332
> in modern English by H. W. WELLS

INTRODUCTION

AN ABILITY to estimate the age of buildings is of value in distinguishing the phases of growth in settlements. Recognition of the features by which buildings may be dated heightens an awareness of the appearance of individual buildings, and of the character of the settlements they compose. It also draws the attention to the use of local materials and local styles, and as a corollary the growth of communications by means of which both building materials and building styles entered the district. All of these themes, concerned with the explanatory description of settlements, are of relevance to the geographer, for whom this introductory paper is intended. It is an introduction to a complex subject in which few generalizations of proven validity as yet exist, so that it must be used critically. It is also an introduction to a relatively new subject in which much fundamental data remain to be established, and to which geographers by discovering and recording, and by studying regional distributions, are well able to contribute.

The age of the existing buildings is obviously not necessarily any indication of when the site was first occupied; several houses may have followed one another on the same site. On the other hand a village with many medieval buildings was manifestly a village in medieval times and this may well be a fact that neither map nor document could otherwise establish. A mention in Domesday Book establishes neither the precise site nor the size of the settlements so mentioned. For many settlements the only evidence of stages in growth or decay is to be found in the buildings of the settlement and this applies as much to the isolated farmstead as to the village and the town in many parts of the country. The majority of houses can be dated with a sufficient degree of accuracy from external features, although there are of course many exceptions.

Most old houses have suffered considerable alterations and it is the oldest dateable feature that gives the key to the age. For example, sash windows were not introduced until the late seventeenth century, but they were subsequently inserted in many older houses. In such houses the general style or the dimensions or detail of the brickwork may well establish its greater age. Many old houses were completely refronted in the eighteenth century but lay-out and roof shape, and particularly a view from the back where earlier details may well survive, will generally betray a greater age. For some houses only an inspection of the internal details, particularly the roof timbers, will permit final dating, but such inspection may not be practicable. These houses, which need to be examined thoroughly before they can contribute to the dating of a settlement pattern, are to be counted the failures of the scheme to be outlined, but taking the country as a whole they are not so numerous as to impair its usefulness. As well as taking note of the occasional failure of the key, the user must also take cognizance of the time lag due to the persistence of local styles and local conservatism. For example, the variations in the Georgian styles, introduced in London and such society centres as Bath and Brighton, appear in remoter areas, if at all, at a later date and often in modified form. The dissemination of such styles owed much to the copy books produced in great numbers from the early eighteenth century, but the application of the ideas contained in the books depended upon the skill of local builders and the materials at their disposal.

For these various reasons this introduction may give only an approximate indication of age, but on the other hand it may stimulate interest in a very large body of evidence that at first sight appears quite intractable. It is essentially a field key and not an authority for ascribing an exact date to a given building.

A. EARLY STONE HOUSES

The oldest surviving stone houses in this country are of two types: (1) first-floor houses, (2) hall houses. In the first and more numerous type, the living room was on the first floor, the ground floor being used for storage. Many of the houses appear to have belonged to merchants, and examples, in various states of repair, exist in Southampton, Chester, Shrewsbury and Lincoln. As town houses they are found only in the larger medieval towns, whilst in the countryside they number about a score, excluding abbots' houses and the like. They are so rare, and so few can remain for discovery, that they are unlikely to constitute a serious problem in settlement studies, but they may be recognized by the original small upstairs windows, either round headed in the 12th century Norman style, or pointed in the 13th century Early English style. Some of them can be distinguished by an outside staircase or by the original first floor doorway.

The hall type house had its living room on the ground floor and was open to the roof timbers, through a hole in which smoke from the central hearth escaped. These houses have a wider date range, and even excluding castle and episcopal halls they are found from the early 13th to the early 16th century. As with houses of other materials, the smaller examples are likely to occur late rather than early within this long period. Most of them, naturally, are in areas of good, easily worked building stone; consequently, in counties such as Gloucestershire and Northamptonshire, where no large-scale surveys have been undertaken, many must await discovery. To date them it is necessary to have some knowledge of the changes in medieval building styles, for which, since it is too complicated a matter to be set out shortly, reference must be made to one of the standard works (see bibliography).

B. TIMBER HOUSES

The houses of the Anglo-Saxons were of timber, and perhaps for the poor, of cob or turf. None has survived, but wooden hall-type houses have been revealed by excavation. The earliest surviving timber houses are aisled halls of the 13th and 14th centuries, but they are rare and occur only in south-east England

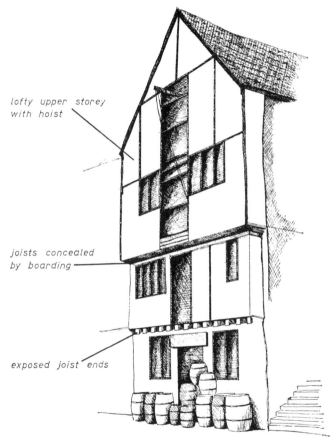

lofty upper storey with hoist

joists concealed by boarding

exposed joist ends

FIG. 1.
32 Close, Newcastle upon Tyne. Timber framed warehouse.

together with east Suffolk. Aisleless timber houses of the 14th century are more numerous and there are very many survivors from the 15th and 16th centuries, even in districts with good building stone, especially in towns.

Timber was gradually superseded as a building material by brick and stone, beginning in the late 16th century, but in places where it was readily available it persisted in use for the smaller farmhouses and cottages into the second half of the 18th century. Timber-framed houses are very common in southern England, excluding the south-west, where they are found only in towns; also in the Midlands and East Anglia, although in the Cotswolds again they exist only

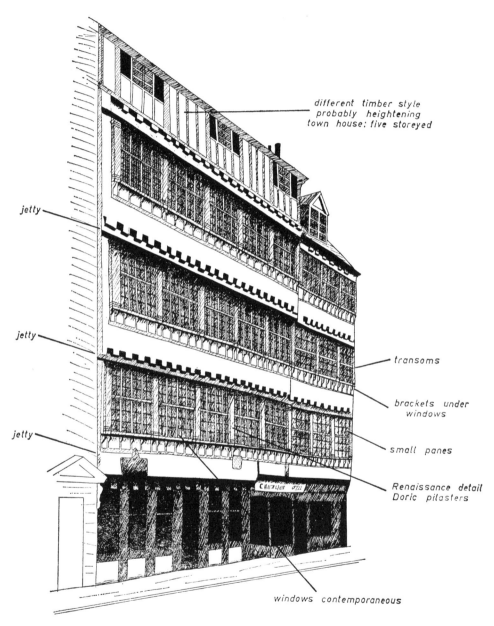

different timber style
probably heightening
town house: five storeyed

jetty

jetty

transoms

brackets under
windows

jetty

small panes

Renaissance detail
Doric pilasters

windows contemporaneous

FIG. 2.
Surtees House and 37 Sandhill, Newcastle upon Tyne.

in the towns. North of the Trent they are less common and outside the towns good quality timberwork appears, generally speaking, in manor houses or their equivalent, rather than farmhouses. In Lincolnshire and Lancashire there are considerable numbers of houses built of such poor quality timber that they were disguised from the first by plaster; though difficult to date, they appear on present knowledge to be mainly of the 17th century. In the four northern counties there are virtually no timber-framed houses save for some late examples in towns, the most notable being in Newcastle upon Tyne (Figs. 1 and 2). One qualification must be made about timber houses in towns. Wherever in England

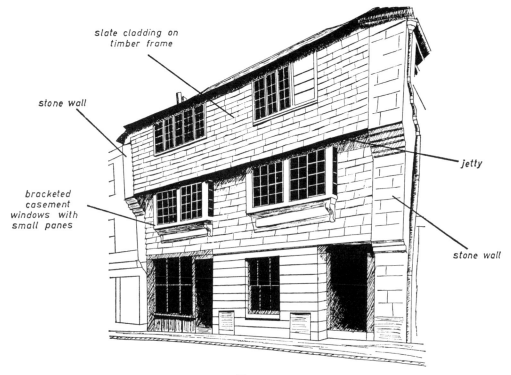

FIG. 3.
11 High Street, Launceston. Three-quarter house.

and Wales there was good building stone, it was used to provide fireproof walls between houses, and in many cases it seems to have been used for the back wall too, so that only the jettied front was actually of timber. There are many examples of this style, the "three-quarters house", in the south-west (Fig. 3).

The structural use of wood was therefore in vogue for centuries, and in this long period of time, various technical developments took place which altered the appearance of the house. For example, the earliest timber houses were, with few exceptions, open to the roof with a central hearth, although this was probably used little for cooking, which was normally done in a detached building. In south-east England and East Anglia these early houses, built before the middle of the 14th century, were aisled, the roof coming low. Improvements in roof construction led to higher walls, the disappearance of aisles and a higher roof. In the 16th century brick chimneys replaced the roof opening and glass began to be used extensively for windows. An added complexity is the existence of various traditions of timber building. In western England and the Midlands during the middle ages the *cruck* house had its roof timbers supported directly from the ground, while in larger and more sophisticated forms the cruck appears as a *base-cruck* in which the blades of the cruck, instead of meeting at the ridge, were joined by a collar beam (Figs. 4 and 5). In the south-east the traditions of the so-called box-frame developed; as the name implies it was a box-like framework in which the entire roof weight was distributed evenly along the supporting walls. It was not a technique used for houses of poor folk*

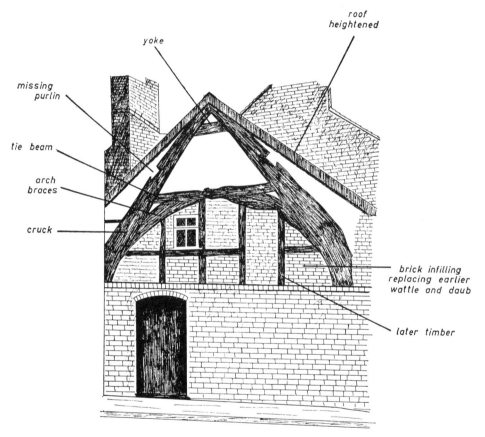

Fig. 4.
Frankwell, Shrewsbury. Cruck cottage.

* The poor man in the quotation from *Piers Ploughman* in the introduction had been driven from his home by
    (1) his wife's tongue;
    (2) the roof covering blowing off and letting in water;
    (3) smoke, due to combination of lack of chimney and green wood.

although (and this tends to be a general problem) surviving examples may have subsequently become labourers' cottages (Fig. 6). Whereas aisled construction died out completely in south-east England by about 1400, except for barns, the cruck method persisted in farmhouses well into the 16th century, and in Lancashire and the north-west for at least a hundred years longer. These parts of England also developed a method of building which dispensed with ground-based roof supports and instead relied solely on the exterior walls; it is known as post and truss construction, the roof weight being concentrated on triangular frames called trusses and transmitted to the ground by their supporting posts.

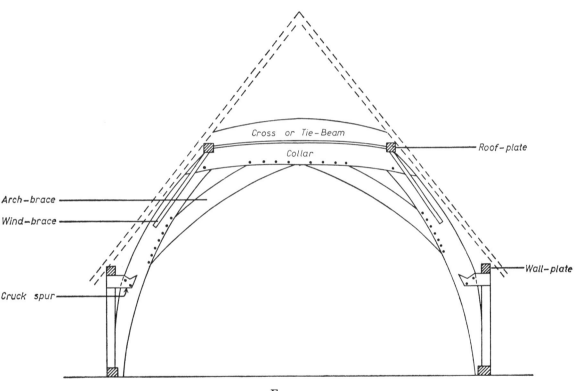

FIG. 5.
Base cruck.

In plan, the most marked distinction is between houses of the feudal ruling class, and those of the peasants. A very few manor houses remain which were built as halls and nothing more, that is to say the surviving building was originally only the principal one of a group of buildings. In the course of time the functions of these lesser structures came to be performed in a single unified house. The first development was to accommodate a buttery and pantry under the roof of the hall. Then a solar or private chamber was added at the other (and it is to this to which Piers Ploughman refers).* These additions were often developed into wings, the plan of the house becoming an "H", and finally in the course of the 16th century the kitchen was incorporated. A regional variant of this development is to be seen in the Wealden house. The solar and service wings were jettied, and the hall, which occupied a lesser proportion of the ground floor space than in contemporary houses in other regions, had recessed eaves. Hall and wings were of equal height, with a single overall roof (Fig. 7). Peasant houses, which were as often of rubble, sod or cob as timber, had, in most of England except the south-east, a single room (the hall) to which was

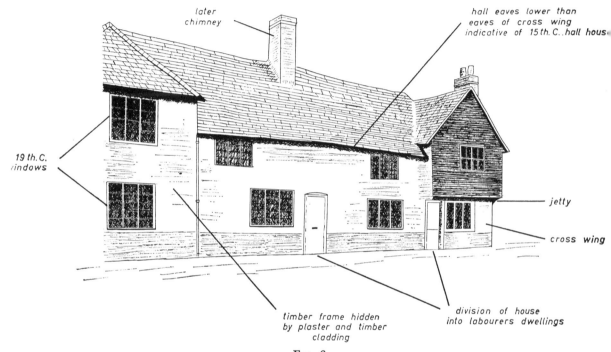

later chimney

hall eaves lower than eaves of cross wing indicative of 15th. C. hall house

19th. C. windows

jetty

cross wing

timber frame hidden by plaster and timber cladding

division of house into labourers dwellings

Fig. 6.
Shere, Surrey. Sub-divided hall house.

attached a byre, the two being undivided structurally. They were improved by adding first a pantry and then a parlour (at that time a bedroom) at the upper end away from the byre. The tendency to separate house and byre, which

* Woe is the hall in all times and seasons
Where neither lord nor lady likes to linger
Now each rich man has a rule to eat in secret,
In a private parlour, for poor folks comfort,
In a chamber with a chimney, perhaps, and leave the chief assembly
Which was made for man to have meat and meals in:
And all to spare to spend what another will spend afterwards.
Vision of Piers Ploughman
Passus X, lines 98–104
in modern English by H. W. Wells.

became more frequent from the 16th century onwards, is reflected in the bipartite appearance of many houses in which neither part is complete in itself.

B(1)   The timber-framed houses of the second half of the 14th century are to be distinguished therefore by differences between the eaves' line of the wings and the hall, where wings, either original or added, exist. The timbering outside south-east England is usually *arch-braced*, sometimes with cusping (Fig. 8), whereas in the south-east, *tension braces* (Fig. 9) are usual and close-studding begins. Doors have square frames but the opening usually used was of the pointed Early English type. This type of doorway persisted to the end of the 15th century.

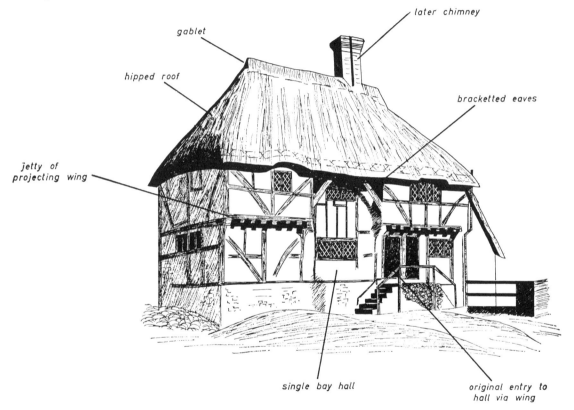

FIG. 7.
The Old Ship, Bignor, Sussex. Wealden type house.*

B(2)   In the 15th century the tension brace gradually became dominant and the eaves line more nearly level as the hall was cleared of supporting timbers. (This development in the exterior corresponds to the internal development of hammer beams or other single span roofs such as those with tie beams.) The wings are usually jettied. Doors are square framed but may have ogee curve lintels.

* With acknowledgement to R. T. Mason.

B(3) In the late 15th and early 16th centuries the external timber was *close-studded* at the front in houses of any pretensions (Fig. 9). The bressummer, the horizontal timber at the base of the projecting upper storey, was frequently richly carved. Houses with a continuous jetty necessarily had an original chimney stack. The two storeyed wings of open halls often had an original chimney stack at the side. The roof was in one span and the eaves line continuous (or nearly so) as in the Wealden house.

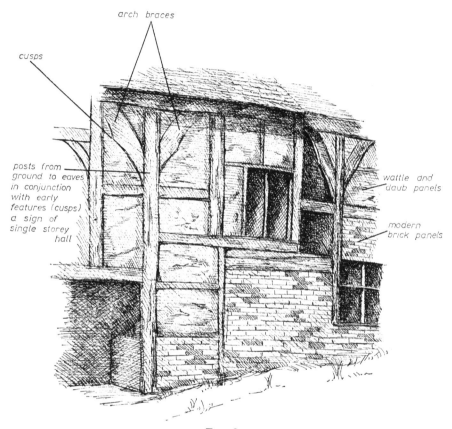

FIG. 8.
House behind Nags' Head, Wyle Cop, Shrewsbury.

B(4) In the late 16th and early 17th centuries (Elizabethan-Jacobean times) the timber house was increasingly embellished with ornamental details such as diagonal struts, often in herring-bone pattern, and "star" framing, none of which had a structural role. This is a regional taste more common in the West Midlands than elsewhere but only East Anglia is entirely without it (Fig. 10). The chimney stack permitted more use of the area above the hall, since by clearing the roof space of smoke it enabled an upper floor to be incorporated throughout the house. Where a central stack has been added to an older house a difference in floor line between wings and centre is usually visible. In south-east England, East Anglia and parts of the Midlands a common type of house has three rooms, two of them being heated by a large internal chimney, with the front door opening into a lobby beside the stack. A smaller version has only the two heated rooms. A very rough and ready guide to the dating of both types is that the earlier ones tend to have one storey and attics whilst the later examples have two storeys, or two storeys and attics. Though these plans are commonest in timber they do occur in stone or brick houses as well.

B(5)   Later in the 17th century decoration became more restrained and timber more sparingly used in large quadrangles (Fig. 11).

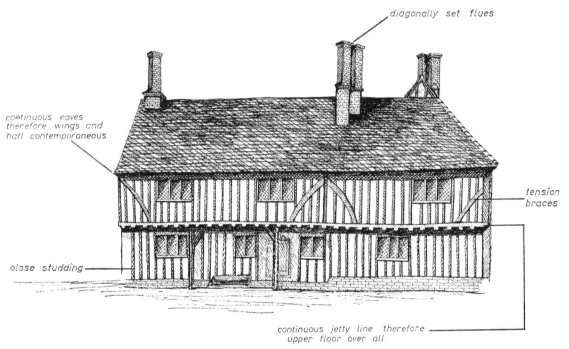

diagonally set flues

continuous eaves therefore wings and hall contemporaneous

tension braces

close studding

continuous jetty line therefore upper floor over all

FIG. 9.
Bushes, Magdalen Laver, Essex.

Windows throughout the period of frame building were casement style with wood mullions. The earliest windows were small, unglazed openings closed by shutters, but when in the late 16th century glass became cheaper, large windows often projecting, part glazed, part shuttered and supported by carved brackets, came into use (Fig. 12). Since in the timber frame house the infill between the principal posts was not load-bearing, glass could be extensively used once it was relatively cheap, but it was normally incorporated in small pieces leaded together (Fig. 2).

In 1784, 1789 and 1803 taxes were levied on bricks and this led once more to an extensive use of a timber frame. Such houses of the late 18th century and early 19th century are common in the south-east. Because the timber was soft wood and mechanically sawn, as compared with the oak used in earlier timber houses, the frame was clad in weatherboarding (Fig. 13). Pseudo half timber, or *stockbrokers' tudor*, in which the timber plays no structural role and is purely imitative of earlier styles with exposed framing, became common from 1850 onwards. This type of timbering can be distinguished by its machine-cut surface, or by being either bolted or nailed on, rather than fastened with wooden pegs. Many older houses have, however, been repaired so that machined timber can be mixed with older wood. An additional way of distinguishing old from new wood is that some old timbers have carpenters'

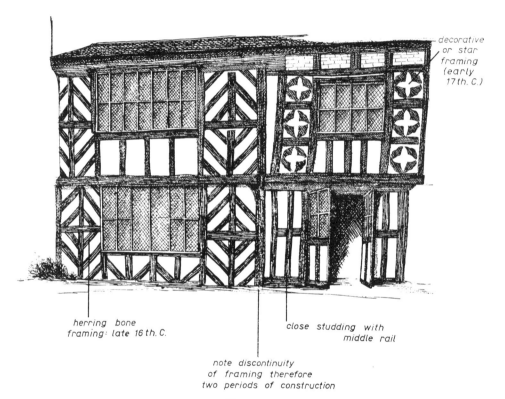

decorative or star framing (early 17th. C.)

herring bone framing: late 16 th. C.

close studding with middle rail

note discontinuity of framing therefore two periods of construction

Fig. 10.
Manor House, Albright Hussey, Salop.

numbers cut into them in order to assist in assembling the frame when it was taken from the yard to be erected on site. One other important difficulty arises with timber houses, when, as commonly happens in East Anglia, they are thoroughly disguised with plaster and little if any timber is visible. Generally the shape and in particular the jettying when it exists is a sufficient means of identification. This problem also applies particularly to the 17th century houses of Lancashire and Lincolnshire to which reference has been made (Fig. 14).

C. BRICK HOUSES

Brick houses became numerous in the 16th century, and brick has remained a building material of importance ever since, although the fashion for stone in Georgian and Regency times led to its being rendered with *stucco*, which was particularly important in the period 1810 to 1850. Also the taxes on bricks in the late eighteenth century led, as already noted, to the re-development of wood buildings. During the long period of their use as a building material the sizes and manner of laying bricks have changed, so too has the taste in the colour of the brickwork. The earliest bricks, some of them imports from Flanders, were about one-and-a-half inches thick. By the 15th century the size rose to 2 inches and in 1571 the size was fixed by statute to $2\frac{1}{4}$ inches. At the

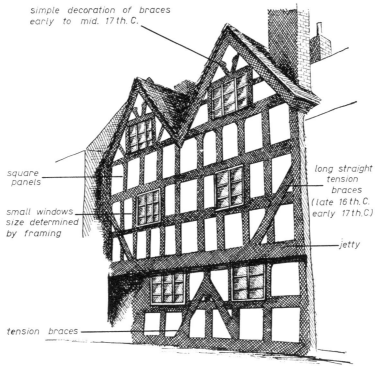

simple decoration of braces
early to mid. 17th. C.

square panels

small windows size determined by framing

long straight tension braces (late 16th.C. early 17th.C)

jetty

tension braces

FIG. 11.
56 St. Mary's Street, Bridgnorth, Salop.

end of the 17th century, $2\frac{1}{2}$ inches was common, and at the end of the 18th century 3 inches was reached because of the brick tax (levied on number irrespective of size). Sixteenth century bricks and bricks of earlier origin had many irregularities; consequently the mortar was thickly laid to produce regular courses. Colours were generally red or plum varied by the use of *flared headers*, bricks burnt to higher temperatures and having a bluish or glassy appearance which were then used to form diaper patterns (Fig. 15). In the 17th century the use of *rubbed* brick gradually developed to achieve regularity and permit very thin mortar joints. The *gauged* work, used to form arches above the windows and doors, and in the quoins, was in a softer brick and usually a bright orange colour. In the 18th century a taste for quieter colours, yellow or grey, developed in London, whilst the corresponding changes in southern England led to the abandonment of flared headers. Up to about 1750 in southern England, flared headers had been much used for fronts, leaving red brick for the window jambs and other details. In East Anglia, for nearly a hundred years beginning about 1770, there was a fondness for pale grey bricks called *Suffolk whites*. These developments came to an end in Victorian times, especially in the period 1850 to 1870 when garish and contrasting colours were used.

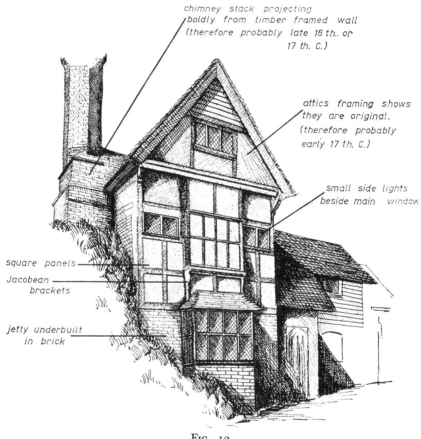

chimney stack projecting boldly from timber framed wall (therefore probably late 16 th.. or 17 th. C.)

attics framing shows they are original. (therefore probably early 17 th. C.)

small side lights beside main window

square panels

Jacobean brackets

jetty underbuilt in brick

Fig. 12.
Penshurst, Kent.

C(1) *15th and 16th century.* Late medieval brick houses do not generally differ in their plan from contemporary stone or timber buildings having an open hall with adjoining service rooms on the ground floor. The brickwork shows many irregularities with thick mortar courses, and is generally a deep red. Windows, where the originals survive, are mullioned and casement. The bond used in the brickwork is generally English but often quite irregular. Chimney stacks in gauged or carved bricks are highly decorative and prominent, but many stacks having this appearance are in fact much later. Bay windows are also important, often one above the other, lighting the hall and the main chamber above it, the whole being an *oriel*. Roofs were always single span, since the houses remained of limited depth; they were normally gabled and indeed a feature of the Elizabethan and Jacobean house whatever its material is often a multiplicity of gables arising from a desire to use the roof space. In Elizabethan times renaissance influences, coming generally from the Low Countries and Germany rather than direct from Italy, began to affect first the very large houses, the small houses later and less. These influences are to be seen in the decorative motifs, not in the plan.

modillioned eaves: cornice

weather boarding

FIG. 13.
Baker Street, Enfield, Middlesex.

C(2)   *17th century.* The adoption of the classical renaissance styles in layout as well as in motifs began with the work of Inigo Jones, in the 1620s, and derived from the word of *Palladio* (1518–1580). The ideal was a symmetrical building with central entrance, giving access to a hall with stairway, the hall giving access to the main rooms. The tradition of the hall as the main room of the house then came to an end, although it lingered in the North to 1700. Symmetry was also achieved by placing the service rooms under the main living room and illuminating them from an area. Servants' sleeping quarters were in the attic and the back stairs became the route to work for the servants. The greater depth of the house led to a double span roof, often hipped.

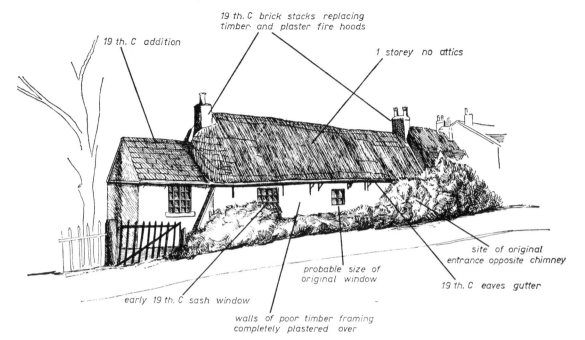

FIG. 14.
60 Gores Lane, Formby, Lancs.

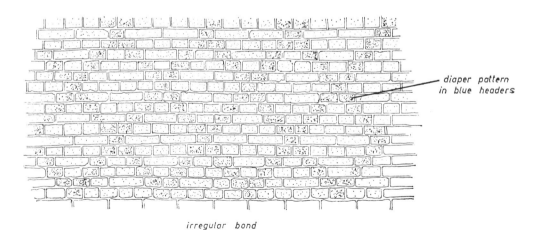

FIG. 15.
Diaper pattern brickwork. Lincoln's Inn, W.C.2.

The brickwork of these houses, which were symmetrical where space allowed, was red and plum colour but becoming increasingly regular. Diaper patterns of blue headers and red stretchers, to which reference has been made, were popular. Flemish bond was adopted. The arches were made up of *voussoirs*, red wedge shaped bricks rubbed to shape with very thin mortar courses. Quoins are also usually rubbed brick but are occasionally rusticated stone. Windows continued to be mullioned, often with transoms as well, with one or more casements, and were often made of wood. By 1680 sash windows appeared and were widely adopted, replacing mullion windows in many older buildings. The whole of the timber of the window frame was visible from the outside, being flush with, or projecting beyond, the brickwork, the windows being flat topped. Glass was

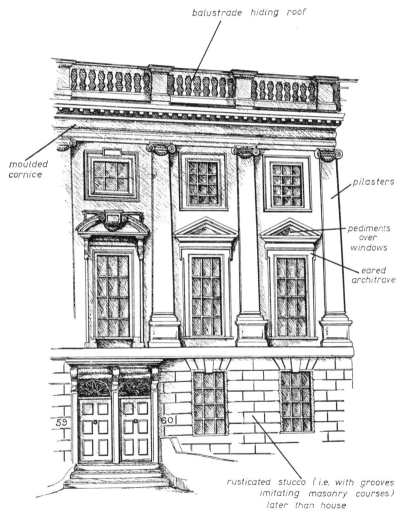

FIG. 16.
59–60 Lincoln's Inn, W.C.2.

still obtainable only in relatively small pieces so that many glazing bars, which were up to 2 inches thick, divided the windows.

Classical motifs derived mainly from Italian sources were used in a relatively small number of great houses, i.e. they were derived from Palladio with the intention of reproducing exactly the details of classical architecture. Smaller houses, many more in number, used classical themes more freely.

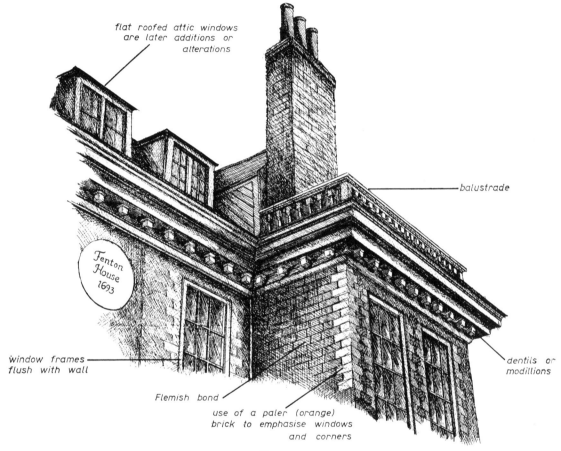

FIG. 17.
Fenton House, Hampstead, N.W.3.

The classicism is to be seen in the *pilasters*, often going to the upper storey (Fig. 16). Another distinguishing feature is the eaves cornice, normally constructed of wood and either dentilled or finished with a concave plastered surface called a cove (Fig. 17). In the late 17th and early 18th century symmetry was often heightened by emphasizing the centre of the facade either by a heavy door case or by a pediment to the window above it.

Besides the houses which came fairly close to the classical canon a fairly large number of houses in south-east England have vigorous brickwork details

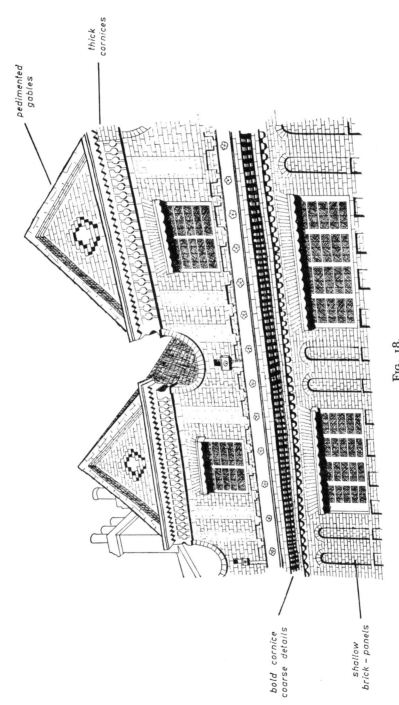

FIG. 18.
High Street, Godalming, Surrey.

including simple classical motifs such as pilasters and round windows, along with bold dentilled string courses and moulded cornices (Fig. 18). This style, once quite common in the towns of Surrey, had its counterparts elsewhere. One such is in south Lancashire where there are houses in which the striking contrasts of the earlier "black and white" timber houses are to some extent perpetuated by sunk panels filled with white plaster; projecting headers were used to form geometrical patterns or the date of erection and the owner's initials, and plastered brick mullions were the rule for windows. These local styles are largely confined to the third quarter of the 17th century, but elsewhere, and generally rather later, the use of prominent brick string courses or a brick architrave to frame the main doorway is a mild reflection of this phase of taste,

heavy brickwork surround   wrought iron work

FIG. 19.
2 King's Bench Walk, Temple, W.C.2.

which corresponds to the contemporary fondness for bold, vigorous detailing in sculpture and woodwork, and declines with it (Fig. 19).

The window tax, first imposed in 1697, continued to be levied until 1851, so that it is mainly houses built before the latter date which will show the window bricked up to avoid duty. This feature, which unfortunately has become associated with the Queen Anne style, is as often due to internal re-arrangement, particularly the introduction of corridors. Even more unfortunately such blocked windows are confused with dummy openings intended to produce symmetry. Wrought iron gates and rails came into fashion late in the century (Fig. 20).

FIG. 20.
Wrought iron gate, Temple, W.C.2.

C(3)   *18th century.* This century shows a continuous decline from the vigorous emphasis of late 17th century work to a thin and refined detail sparingly used, a change corresponding firstly to the rise of Lord Burlington's school of architects proclaiming close adherence to Palladio's classicism, and secondly its decline in favour of the brothers Adam and their followers who used true classical detail copied from Herculaneum and Pompeii. Pattern books rapidly disseminated the ideas of leading architects in the provinces.

Legislation to prevent fire also had its effect on buildings, first in London, later in the provinces. The eaves' cornice disappeared for this reason, being replaced by a parapet, and window frames in London's new buildings after

FIG. 21.
59 Lincoln's Inn, W.C.2.

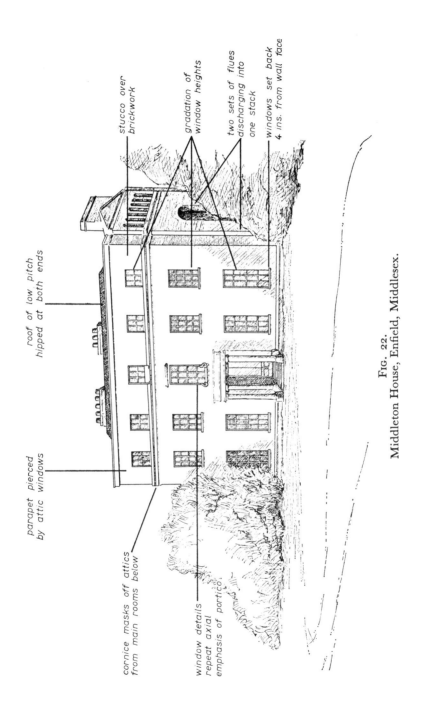

stucco over brickwork

gradation of window heights

two sets of flues discharging into one stack

windows set back 4 ins. from wall face

roof of low pitch hipped at both ends

parapet pierced by attic windows

cornice masks off attics from main rooms below

window details repeat axial emphasis of portico

FIG. 22.
Middleton House, Enfield, Middlesex.

1709 were set back 4 inches. By 1774 as a result of further fire legislation, the sash boxes of windows had to be concealed and all these features gradually became general in towns throughout England, and to a lesser extent in farm-houses.

In town houses, the smaller country houses and the larger farm-houses, changes in style took the same course as in the great houses. Early in the 18th century windows tended to be tall, narrow and quite close together, their heads being often shallow segmental arches; storeys were divided by bands of project-ing bricks or moulded cornices; the eaves projected boldly, either with modil-lions or coves; and between the windows were bands of blue or flared headers, this last being largely confined to southern England. Doorways commonly had big projecting hoods which were either curved or flat and were carried on

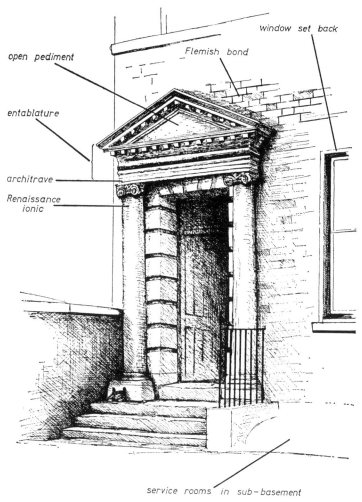

FIG. 23.
15 Lincoln's Inn, W.C.2.

carved brackets (Fig. 21) while in a symmetrical front the centre line was often stressed by special treatment of the window over the doorway, although this feature was also used at a later date (Fig. 22). Just as the parapet replaced the wooden eaves' cornice, so gradually the other emphatic divisions of the frontage fell out of favour. Windows have "flat-arch" heads, cornices became simpler, brick bands were no longer used, and the brickwork itself got paler and blue

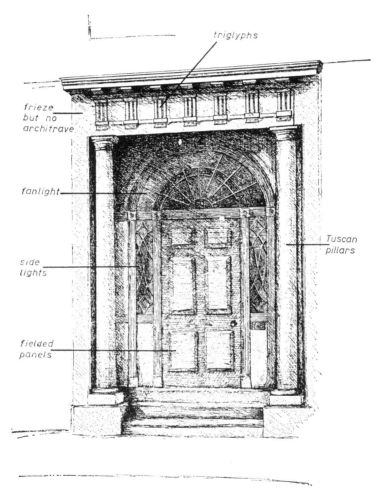

FIG. 24.
Carey Street, W.C.2.

headers disappeared. A precise chronology of these changes can only be established locally and fortunately the existence in many towns and country districts of a series of houses bearing dates, either inscribed on keystones, cast on the lead rainwater heads, or picked out in blue headers, makes this relatively easy. This also gives a guide to the changes in the doorways, often combined with an internal porch, which replaced the Queen Anne type of door-hood.

They may have pillars and an entablature; engaged pilasters; or, in the second half of the century, a broken pediment with a fanlight. As the century progressed, improved solutions to the difficulty of lighting the entrance hall of a house two rooms in depth led to other changes in the appearance of doorways; from a narrow rectangular window over the door (Fig. 23) the fanlight gradually developed into a highly ornamental feature and, where it was wide enough, the hall could be lit instead by windows flanking the front door (Fig. 24).

Towards the end of the century Welsh slate began to appear in many parts of the country, making possible roofs of a lower pitch than had been used hitherto and enabling the old attics within the roof space to be transformed into

FIG. 25.
Fair Oak, Habin, near Rogate, Sussex.

a top storey, albeit often a low one, at no great extra cost. Bow windows came into favour in southern England, notably in the seaside towns from Sussex to Cornwall.

Decorative iron work attached to the buildings as balconies and occasionally as porches became important from 1770 onwards.

C(4) *19th century.* In the early part of the century, the Regency period, three style developments competed with classical vernacular. The Adam brothers had introduced some Greek themes, as well as those deriving from Pompeii and

Herculaneum, but in the early 19th century a deliberate and more correct revival took place. The two phases of the Greek revival, the first being eclectic (Fig. 25) and decorative, the second archaeologically more correct and seeking to produce whole buildings in the style, were repeated with exaggerated effect in the more lasting Gothic revival. It, too, began in the late 18th century, and during the period of about sixty years for which it persisted, the classical proportions and planning of houses was hardly changed, but pointed casement windows reappeared, together with battlements and drip mouldings over the windows, all being generally of early Tudor inspiration (Fig. 26). Then in the

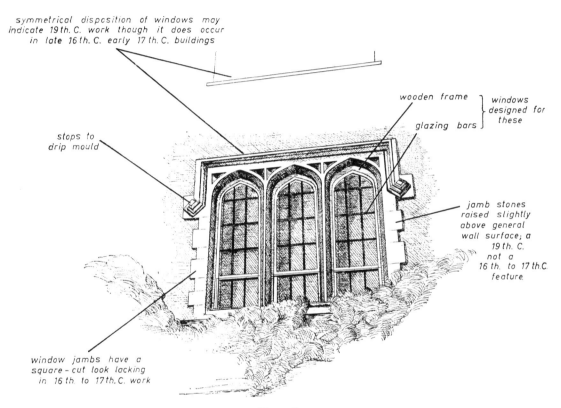

FIG. 26.
New Grove House, Hampstead, N.W.3.

late 1830s, parallelling the ecclesiastical application of an archaeologically correct Gothic, came the building of medieval-looking houses in stone, timber and even brick. Not only country houses both large and small, but also suburban villas, estate cottages and lodges were built in the various medieval styles or free mixtures of them. Roughly contemporary with the Gothic revival came a renewed interest in the Italian renaissance, which for a time had considerable effect on the appearance of the larger suburban houses.

Houses not affected by these styles had recessed doors with narrow columns.

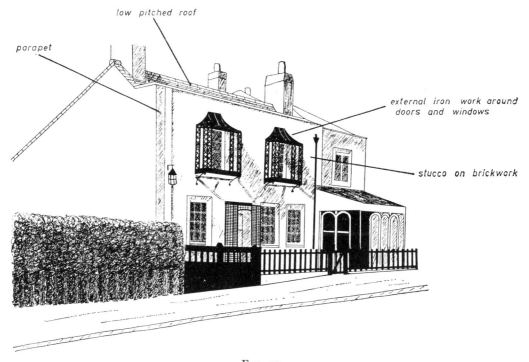

FIG. 27.
Brigadier Hill, Enfield, Middx.

FIG. 28.
Old Cottage, Forty Hill, Enfield, Middlesex.

Symmetry was still maintained with bow or bay windows and the basement service rooms. Glazing bars became thin and the sash window remained. Iron grills were often attached to the sills of the upper windows and external pelmets were employed (Fig. 27). Roofs of low pitch with a covering of Welsh slate brought boldly overhanging eaves back into fashion, with the earlier inconvenience of rain water dripping from them removed by the use of cheap iron gutters (Fig. 28). Stucco either over the lower storey or over the whole of the house was widely employed.

The early 19th century also saw a considerable growth of suburban villa

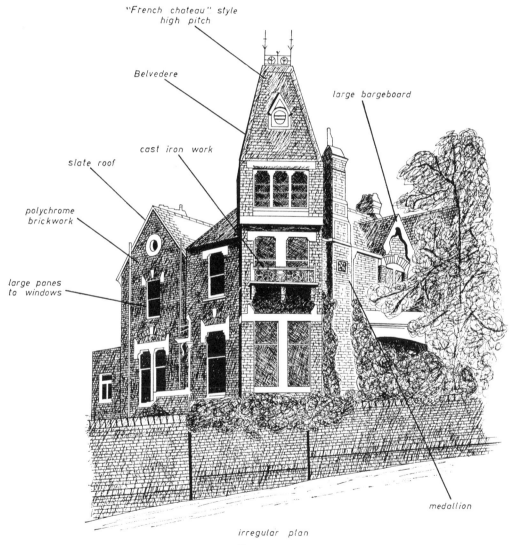

FIG. 29.
Prince Arthur Road, Hampstead, N.W.3.

building as the centres of cities lost their residential character. Terraced houses were widely employed in built-up areas or industrial areas for cheapness, the basements being used for service rooms or coal storage. This mode of building had first been used in the late 17th century in Red Lion Square, London. Semi-detached houses, a type of building that contributes much to the English landscape, also appeared in the late 18th century and became increasingly widespread in the 19th century.

By the middle of the century a revolt was in full swing against classicism generally whether of the careful neo-Greek or the Italianate variety. The

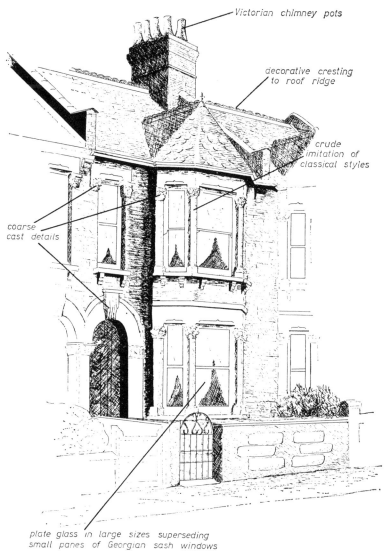

FIG. 30.
South Street, Enfield, Middlesex.

Gothic revival was a manifestation of it, but everywhere symmetry was abandoned for a broken line with numerous gables to which a great mixture of styles contributed, including Byzantine and French. Many large villas were equipped with belvederes or towers (Fig. 29). Improvements in glass, which became increasingly cheap after it was first rolled in 1838, led to large conservatories becoming part of the upper-middle class villa and later, to a vogue of stained glass in doors and windows. Houses for the poor in the large cities were in part decayed dwellings once occupied by the middle classes, or to an ever increasing extent built by industrialists for their work people. The Public Health Act of 1875 first enforced minimum standards and large areas of Victorian working-class dwellings were completed to these; they were usually narrow single-front terrace houses, with mullion windows, the mullions often

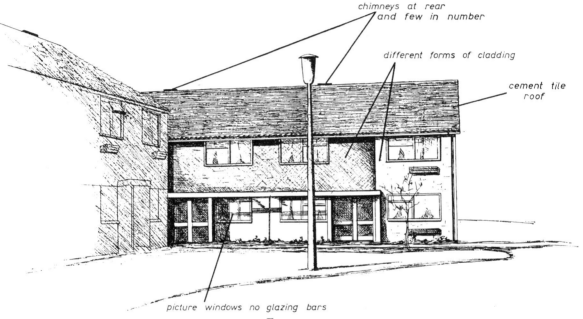

FIG. 31.
Cheviot Close, Enfield, Middlesex.

treated as attached columns, and perhaps with dentilations or brackets under the eaves (Fig. 30). By the end of the century rather quieter styles returned. The first large blocks of flats for working people constructed by various trusts were built in London in 1868. Throughout the century Welsh slate roofs were widely employed and the mechanization of brick manufacture led in the 1850s to 1860s to very regular standardized bricks. Flettons appeared in 1889.

C(5) *20th century*. The quieter modes of the late 19th century continued into the Edwardian period, but with a growing use of clay tile instead of slate. The semi-detached house continued to spread and dominated the growth of suburban districts in the inter-war years. Georgian, Queen Anne and neo-

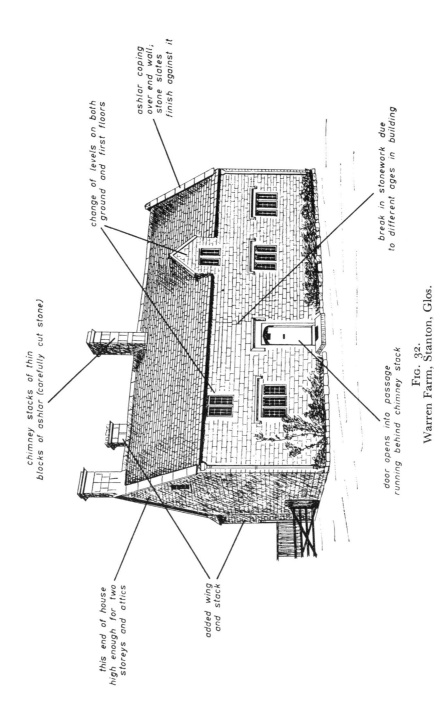

ashlar coping
over end wall;
stone slates
finish against it

change of levels on both
ground and first floors

break in stonework due
to different ages in building

chimney stacks of thin
blocks of ashlar (carefully cut stone)

door opens into passage
running behind chimney stack

this end of house
high enough for two
storeys and attics

added wing
and stack

Fig. 32.
Warren Farm, Stanton, Glos.

Gothic styles were also employed but generally for public or commercial building. To private building, the Housing Act of 1919 was responsible for adding the council houses, also very much part of the English scene. Semi-detached or in short terraces, often with the same bow windows, these are merely an austere form of the private semi-detached dwelling. The basements had disappeared. Layout is as distinctive as appearance since both private and public buildings were influenced by Ebenezer Howard and the garden city concept. Curving roads, front lawns, flowering cherries, with the names "Chez Nous", "Casa Mia" and "Mon Repos", contrast with the narrow frontage and the tiny or non-existent gardens of the poorer Victorian dwellings. Semi-detached houses continued to spread after the Second World War. Council housing, still cottagey, begins now to end the long domination of brick for small houses by utilizing new materials such as cast concrete blocks, but large blocks of flats became increasingly part of the urban scene. In the private sector, the appearance of central heating has led to the disappearance of all but one of the numerous chimneys and flues of the older houses (Fig. 31). The clay tile is replaced by the cement tile and the garage becomes increasingly part of the house. The large sheet glass windows, the pitch pine decoration and the metal casements, plus the occasional stone-faced house, complete a not very agreeable picture.

D. LATER STONE HOUSES

Despite the popularity of timber-framed houses in the 15th, 16th and 17th centuries, stone never fell entirely out of use. In 16th-century Shropshire, for example, brick, stone and wood were used contemporaneously. In Northumberland defensible stone tower houses (the so-called pele houses) and two-storied part-vaulted houses called bastles were built up to the late 16th century. In many districts with good building stone, especially those south of the Trent, stone houses appear to become numerous for the first time in the 16th century, the use of stone gradually superseding wood, until in many areas it was replaced in turn by brick, but even in clay districts stone building was of social significance especially in the early 19th century, when it was copied in stucco. Stone buildings of this later period, unlike the medieval houses already mentioned, were often in *ashlar*, that is, large smooth regular blocks of stone permitting regular courses. Such material when hand cut was costly, and its rare appearance in farm houses is an indication of a late 18th century or 19th century date. In larger houses it is general from Elizabethan times.

For the larger houses, where defence was no longer important, many of the construction details (and therefore the evidence for dating) are similar whatever the structural material employed. Tudor or Elizabethan manor houses are recognizably Tudor or Elizabethan in stone or brick. The gables and the large mullion windows appear in various materials and in widely separated localities as in Trerice near Newlyn in Cornwall, Langley House, Rogate, Sussex, both in stone, Sawston Hall, Cambridgeshire, in clunch, and Ingatestone, Essex, in brick. The classical influence towards symmetry, as distinct from motifs, appears in stone buildings in Shropshire in the 1680s, in Northumberland in the late 1660s, forty to fifty years after Inigo Jones built Queen's House, Greenwich. This time lag, at the most fifty years, must be borne constantly in mind when

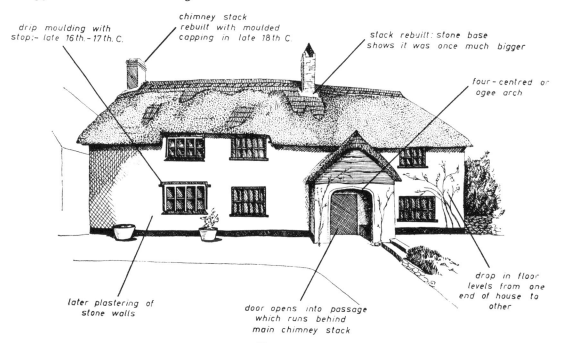

chimney stack
rebuilt with moulded
capping in late 18th C.

drip moulding with
stop:- late 16th.-17th. C.

stack rebuilt: stone base
shows it was once much bigger

four-centred or
ogee arch

later plastering of
stone walls

door opens into passage
which runs behind
main chimney stack

drop in floor
levels from one
end of house to
other

Fig. 33.
Townsend Farm, Stockland, Devon.

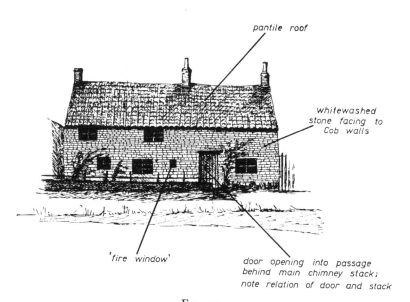

pantile roof

whitewashed
stone facing to
Cob walls

'fire window'

door opening into passage
behind main chimney stack;
note relation of door and stack

Fig. 34.
Rosemarie Cottage, Appleton in the Moors, N. Riding, Yorkshire.†

† With acknowledgement to Miss P. Allerston.

attempting to date houses from the evidence of the external features. It was reduced as improvements in communications took place and the circulation of copy books increased. On the other hand the remoteness of the provinces should not be exaggerated. Stylish innovation took place quickly at the higher social levels so that Trewardine, a stone-built manor house in Constantine in Cornwall, was refaced with ashlar in 1719 and had sash windows added.

It is with the smaller house rather than with the manor house and the large farmhouse that difficulty in dating will be experienced. In Wales and in the west country, and in the south-west, traditional styles lingered. The long single storey house with men and beasts under one roof was still built in the 17th and

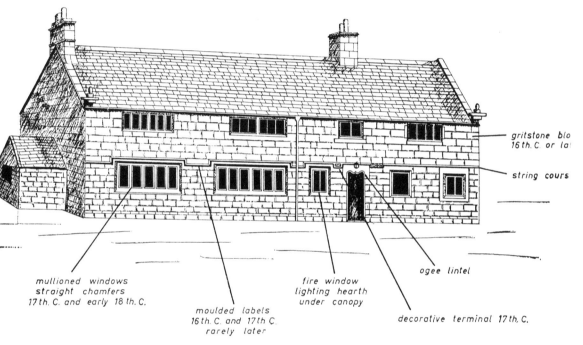

gritstone blo
16th. C. or la

string cours

mullioned windows
straight chamfers
17th. C. and early 18 th. C.

moulded labels
16th. C. and 17th C.
rarely later

fire window
lighting hearth
under canopy

ogee lintel

decorative terminal 17th. C.

FIG. 35.
Hippins, Blackshaw, West Riding, Yorkshire.‡

‡ With acknowledgement to C. F. Stell.

18th centuries. More often, from the 16th century onward, the house and byre were rebuilt in two stages, in the second of which the cows were put into a separate building and the lower end of the house turned to domestic use. This can be clearly seen in Fig. 32 where the break in the masonry coursing and in floor levels reveal two periods of re-building. The curved door lintel, the stone mullions and the drip mouldings are all evidence for a 16th or early 17th century date. The drip mould with stop (i.e. vertical terminations) dies out by the end of the 17th century; plain horizontal drip moulds continue in some districts for another fifty years. Drip moulds come back into vogue again with the Gothic revival (Fig. 26). Similarly, in Fig. 33 the change in floor levels shows the reconstruction, but again the mullions, the flat ogee curve of the porch and the drip moulds are evidence for a 16th or early 17th century date.

Another survivor was the cross or through passage house, a two-storied derivative of the hall house still built in Yorkshire in the 18th century, with the fire or inglenook window as a means of identification (Fig. 34). Other small houses had the door opening direct into the living room and a bedroom loft reached by ladder was at one end. Such houses are often built of rubble or cob (see below) and thatched or with stone slates. Some have a continuous string course in place of separate drip moulds and this is an indication everywhere of

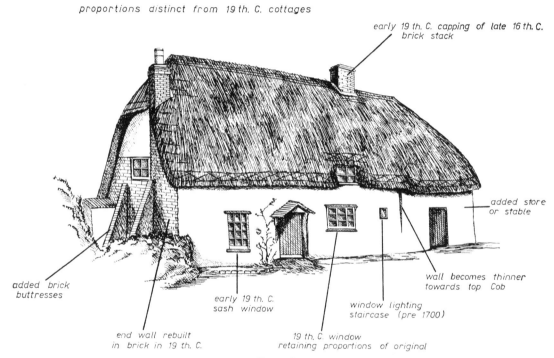

proportions distinct from 19 th. C. cottages

early 19 th. C. capping of late 16 th. C. brick stack

added store or stable

added brick buttresses

wall becomes thinner towards top Cob

early 19 th. C. sash window

window lighting staircase (pre 1700)

end wall rebuilt in brick in 19 th. C.

19 th. C. window retaining proportions of original

Fig. 36.
Harts Cottage, Corfe Mullen, Dorset.

a late 17th century date (Fig. 35). From the early 18th century they had generally two chimneys, one of which heated a parlour, and there was an increasing tendency to make the house symmetrical with the chimneys at the ends. The living room fire was used for cooking and in many cases in the 18th and 19th century, a bread oven was added against the main stack, sometimes as a round projection, often replacing a winding stair. In the 18th century, even in quite lowly dwellings, sash windows became general. Late in the same century, the *mansard* roof was widely used, as in the Cotswolds, the upper floor being used for storage or lit by dormers for bedrooms. By the 19th century these traditional styles were being lost. Brick became general for the poorer houses. The casement windows re-appeared especially after 1833 when cast iron window frames were marketed for labourers' cottages.

E. COB

Cob is a mixture of clay, chopped straw, small stones and road scrapings, its name being one given to it in Devon. It was sometimes run like concrete between boards, in semi-liquid form, and left to set, and sometimes merely piled up in a thicker mix and later pared down to make a smooth wall face. Whichever method was used, the walls had to be plastered to give protection against the weather, so that the true nature of the material is often hard to recognize. One common indication is that the wall surface often bulges slightly inwards and outwards in an irregular way not found with stone or brick; another arises from the fact that the corners were rarely bonded together, so that brick or stone buttresses have been applied to a great many cob buildings in order to keep the long walls, which take the weight of the roof, upright. Cob, nevertheless, is a highly durable material which seems to occur where there is neither a good building stone nor a tradition of good timber-framed construction. It is best known in Devon and Dorset, where it can be found in farmhouses of the late 16th (Fig. 36) to 19th centuries, while at least one cob building with late medieval detail is known. Such buildings may perhaps be dated approximately by other features, as in the examples given. Elsewhere cob has been less often recognized for what it is. A recent study has shown that there are still many cob buildings in Northamptonshire, again with a wide dating range. Warwickshire, on the other hand, has many early 19th century cottages of cob, but few, if any, earlier buildings of this material. In the North Riding of Yorkshire and in Devonshire some late 17th century buildings have cob walls with an outer skin of stone, so that the real nature of the walling can only be revealed when the inner surface is exposed, and because this form of construction is so difficult to detect it may well have a much wider distribution. An allied material used in Cambridgeshire and Norfolk is clay lump, which is really a kind of sun-dried brick made in larger sizes than fired brick.

When all the relevant dating criteria have been applied there will still be some houses in which an earlier or different phase of development has to be inferred if they are to make their proper contribution to the study of a settlement pattern. The house depicted in Fig. 37 shows by its mixture of timber-framing and brickwork that it has a complicated history. It looks like either a much-altered H-plan house with two cross-wings, or a T-plan house with one cross-wing placed at right angles to the main range, i.e. at the "upper" end, the one further away from the entrance. The tall brick range is likely on general grounds to be later than the timber-framing on either side of it, and can be dated to about the middle of the 16th century by the blue headers in a diaper pattern. To the left, the close-studded timber framing might, in Warwickshire, be of any date between 1450 and 1550 but since it is at what was socially the more important end of the house (containing the solar), it is unlikely to be contemporary with the brick range, or even nearly so; it may therefore be about 1500 or somewhat earlier. At the right-hand side the curved braces incorporated in a roof truss may well be of the 15th century but could be as late as 1500. Below them the spacing of the framing panels seems unrelated to the

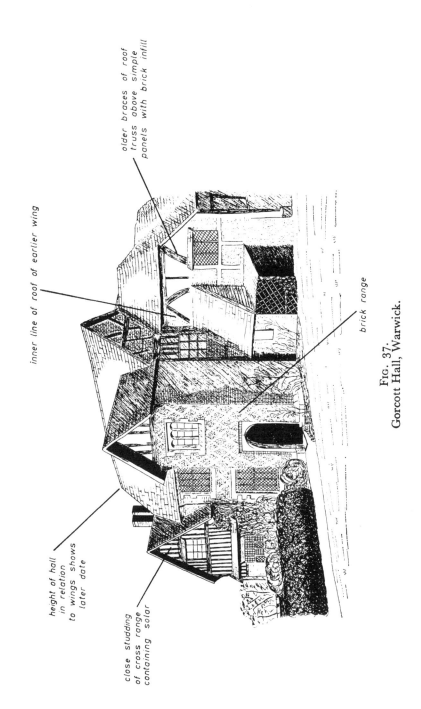

older braces of roof
truss above simple
panels with brick infill

inner line of roof of earlier wing

brick range

height of hall
in relation
to wings shows
later date

close studding
of cross range
containing solar

Fig. 37.
Gorcott Hall, Warwick.

truss above, and, taken with the brick infilling, suggests they are later work. Moreover, the framing at this end of the middle brick-fronted range appears patchy and of more than one period, and the brickwork of the porch is partly covered in plaster as if for an inside wall. These points add up to an earlier wing which once extended forward beyond the brick front of the main range. Having established that there were two timber-framed wings it is now certain that the mid-16th century brick portion of two lofty storeys replaces an earlier and lower timber hall open from floor to roof. As for its date, it must have been at least as old as the oldest work in the wings. To refine the dating beyond this point would entail a thorough examination of the interior, so that in this particular case, the actual date of the earlier house can hardly be advanced by this kind of deductive reasoning beyond the period to which the earliest constructive feature can be ascribed. Nevertheless, in determining the size and form of the earlier house, argument of this kind establishes a point which may often be just as important in settlement studies as the date itself.

SUGGESTIONS FOR FURTHER READING

The best general study of the medieval house is:

Parker, J. H. and Turner, T. H. (1853). *Domestic Architecture of the Middle Ages*. Oxford, J. H. Parker.

For a more detailed study:

Wood, M. (1965). *The English Medieval House*. London, Phoenix.

There are many other texts of value including:

Barley, M. W. (1963). *The House and Home*. London, Vista.
Barley, M. W. (1961). *The English Farm House and Cottage*. London, Routledge & Kegan Paul.
Forrester, H. (1964). *The Smaller Queen Anne and Georgian House*. Essex Record Office, Chelmsford.
Lloyd, N. (1934). *A History of English Brickwork*. Montgomery.
Turner, R. (1952). *The Smaller English House*. London, Batsford.
Wood-Jones, R. B. (1963). *Traditional Domestic Architecture in the Banbury District*. Manchester U.P.

Of great value is "The Buildings of England" series by N. Pevsner (Penguin Books) now available for over half the English counties. The student should also consult papers in various periodicals, for example:

Alcock, N. W. (1962). Houses in an East Devon Parish. *Trans. Devon. Assoc.*, XVIC, 185–232.
Brunskill, R. W. (1962). Clay Houses of Cumberland. *Trans. Ancient Monuments Soc.*, **10**, 57–80.
Sheppard, J. A. (1966). Vernacular buildings in England and Wales: a survey of recent work by architects, archaeologists and social historians. *Trans. Inst. Brit. Geog.*, **40**, 21–37.
Smith, J. T. (1966). Timber framed building in England. *Archaeol. J.*, CXXII, 135–158.

KEY

The following key is to be used in a manner similar to a botanical key. It is, of course, very imperfect, but may have the result of directing attention to specific features of a building. It is intended as a basis for study, to be amended and developed by the student as he or she becomes familiar with the houses of a given district. It could be made more precise for a given district by collation with other dating evidence.

1. *Structure in*

wood (perhaps plastered)	see (A)
brick (perhaps stuccoed or with pebble dash)	see (B)
stone (perhaps stuccoed or with pebble dash)	see (C)
cob	see (D)

(A) *Wood* (a) arch braced   *late 14th century*
                      possible confirmatory evidence: differences in eaves' line
                                doors with "Early English" lintels
                                general "low" dimension
              (b) tension braced   *early–mid 15th century*
                                                              (or earlier in south-east)
                      possible confirmatory evidence: near level eaves' line
                                doors with ogee curve lintels
              (c) close studded   *late 15th, early 16th century*
                      possible confirmatory evidence: carved bressumer
                                eaves' line continuous
              (d) ornamental details ("stars", cusps)   *late 16th, early 17th century*
                      possible confirmatory evidence: overall and level upper
                                floor (as shown by windows and/or jetty)
                                large windows not added to earlier structures, i.e. in
                                unison with the timber structure
              (e) large quadrangles   *17th century*
              (f) weatherboarding   *late 18th, early 19th century*
                      possible confirmatory evidence: contemporaneous sash
                                windows
                                classical motifs
                                symmetry
(B) *Brick* (a) thin brick up to 2¼ inch red, thick mortar, English bond
                                                              16th and early 17th century
                      possible confirmatory evidence: flared headers, diaper pat-
                                terns, classical motifs later rather rather than earlier,
                                prominent chimney stacks, roof one span in buildings
                                of moderate width
              (b) rubbed bricks in quoins and arches often orange, bricks
                                2½ inch   *late 17th, early 18th century*
                      possible confirmatory evidence: heavy brick frame to doors,
                                or pilasters, eaves cornice (superseded by parapet early
                                in 18th century), stone quoins, sash windows with thick
                                glazing bars, whole of sash visible and flush with brick-
                                work
              (c) grey or yellow in London, white in East Anglia, red without
                      blue headers elsewhere   *mid and late 18th, early 19th century*
                                                                       (see 2)
                      possible confirmatory evidence: external pelmets, iron grilles
                                on window sills or around doors, set back sash win-
                                dows, Greek porticos or "Gothic" motifs
              (d) various colours intermixed, flared headers, bright reds with
                      smooth faces in Midlands and North   *mid to late 19th century*
                      possible confirmatory evidence: pointed casement windows,
                                mullioned windows, irregular plan, stained glass, con-
                                servatories, slate roofs, iron gutters

smaller houses narrow single-front
(*f*) "pink" flettons, wire cut rusticated brick
late 19th, 20th centuries
possible confirmatory evidence: clay tiles, no basements, semidetached or terraced, "bathroom" windows, curving roads, front lawns, appearance of materials other than brick, indication of mid 20th century, timber as decoration, i.e. mock tudor
(*g*) pebble dash—as (*f*)

(C) *Stone*   (*a*) rubble or free stone built, fairly low eaves, small arched windows   *medieval*
possible confirmatory evidence: upstairs door, two centred arch to door
(*b*) large, irregular in plan, or E- or H-shaped, large mullioned windows   *16th and early 17th centuries*
possible confirmatory evidence: stopped drip stone mouldings (persisting later in west and north), four centred arches (ogee), string course around chimney
(*c*) small, regular but not symmetrical, small casement or mullioned windows   *16th and 17th centuries*
possible confirmatory evidence: traces of bipartite development (i.e. irregular floors) or through passage (surviving to early 18th century), drip mouldings or continuous string course
(*d*) freestone, mansard roof, dormers   *18th century*
possible confirmatory evidence: mainly in oolite districts
(*e*) large regular, symmetrical, usually with basement, often ashlar in towns   (see 2)
possible confirmatory evidence: classical motifs
(*f*) rubble or freestone, small (2 lower rooms), symmetrical—chimney both ends   *18th century*
possible confirmatory evidence: sash windows, thick glazing bars
(*g*) stuccoed, as (B)(*d*)

(D) *Cob*   (*a*) small casement windows   *16th and 17th centuries*
possible confirmatory evidence: traces of bipartite development, stone chimney stacks, stair window
(*b*) sash windows, brick chimney stacks   *18th and early 19th centuries*
possible confirmatory evidence: traces of classical motifs, i.e. porch details

2.

(*a*) door with pediment and entablatures   *early 18th century*
possible confirmatory evidence: windows round topped or with consols and entablatures
(*b*) door with broken entablature and rounded fanlight
late 18th century
possible confirmatory evidence: thin glazing bars to windows, flat topped windows set back
(*c*) door with "Greek" portico   *early 19th century*
possible confirmatory evidence: windows with raised surrounds and entablatures, external pelmets

NOTES

NOTES

NOTES

NOTES

NOTES

NOTES

NOTES